BLACK HISTORY

LEGENDS ALPHABET

Words by Robin Feiner

Aa

A is for Maya Angelou.
This legendary author, poet, playwright, and activist used her pen to voice Black pride. With classics like 'Still I Rise' and 'I Know Why the Caged Bird Sings,' Angelou was one of the strongest defenders of Black culture.

B

Bb

B is for Ruby Bridges. Six! That's how old this legend was when she broke through the color barrier as the first Black child to attend an all-white school in New Orleans, Louisiana. In 1960, she showed enormous courage and helped pave the way for desegregation in Southern schools.

C is for Bessie Coleman.
In the 1920s, Black women didn't dare dream of becoming pilots. One did. Coleman traveled to France to get her license, returning as America's first Black female pilot. She showed Black children everywhere that the sky's the limit.

D is for Angela Davis.
This legendary author and activist was retrospectively named Time magazine's 1971 Woman of the Year. Her motto? 'I am no longer accepting the things I cannot change. I am changing the things I cannot accept!'

NAACP
Does the Job!
join now

Ee

E is for Medgar **E**vers.
As a boy, he walked 12 miles a day to attend his segregated school. Years later, he became the first NAACP field secretary in Mississippi and fought to end segregation and enforce voting rights.

F is for **F**rederick Douglass.
If the word 'brave' could describe one man, it would be Douglass, who risked it all to gain his freedom from slavery! He wrote a famed autobiography, advised President Lincoln, and became the most legendary Black abolitionist ever.

Gg

G is for Gil Scott-Heron. The 'Godfather of Rap' crafted jazz and poetry that made listeners think about equality and race. Righteous tracks like 'The Revolution Will Not Be Televised' earned him his place in the Rock & Roll Hall of Fame.

H is for **H**arriet Tubman.
Few fought for emancipation like 'Moses.' Born into slavery in 1822, she battled for her freedom and then dedicated her life to doing the same for others. She helped free at least 70 slaves via the Underground Railroad!

Memphis Free Speech

I is for Ida B. Wells.
This legendary journalist told the public of the challenges Black Americans faced in the 1800s. On top of that, she helped found the National Association for the Advancement of Colored People (NAACP)!

B
Dodgers
42

J is for Jackie Robinson.
April 15 is Jackie Robinson Day. On that day in 1947, this legend broke the color barrier and became the first Black man to play in Major League Baseball. Fifty years later, his number 42 was retired across the entire league.

K is for Martin Luther **K**ing, Jr. 'I have a dream!' In 1963, this minister and civil rights activist uttered those legendary words and changed the course of history. He helped usher in the Civil Rights Act, followed by the Voting Rights Act. MLK will never be forgotten.

L is for Langston Hughes. This jazz poet shone a light on the souls of Black Americans. He inspired Black artists and ushered in the Harlem Renaissance. A fellow Black artist said, 'He set a tone, a standard of brotherhood and friendship and cooperation, for all of us to follow.'

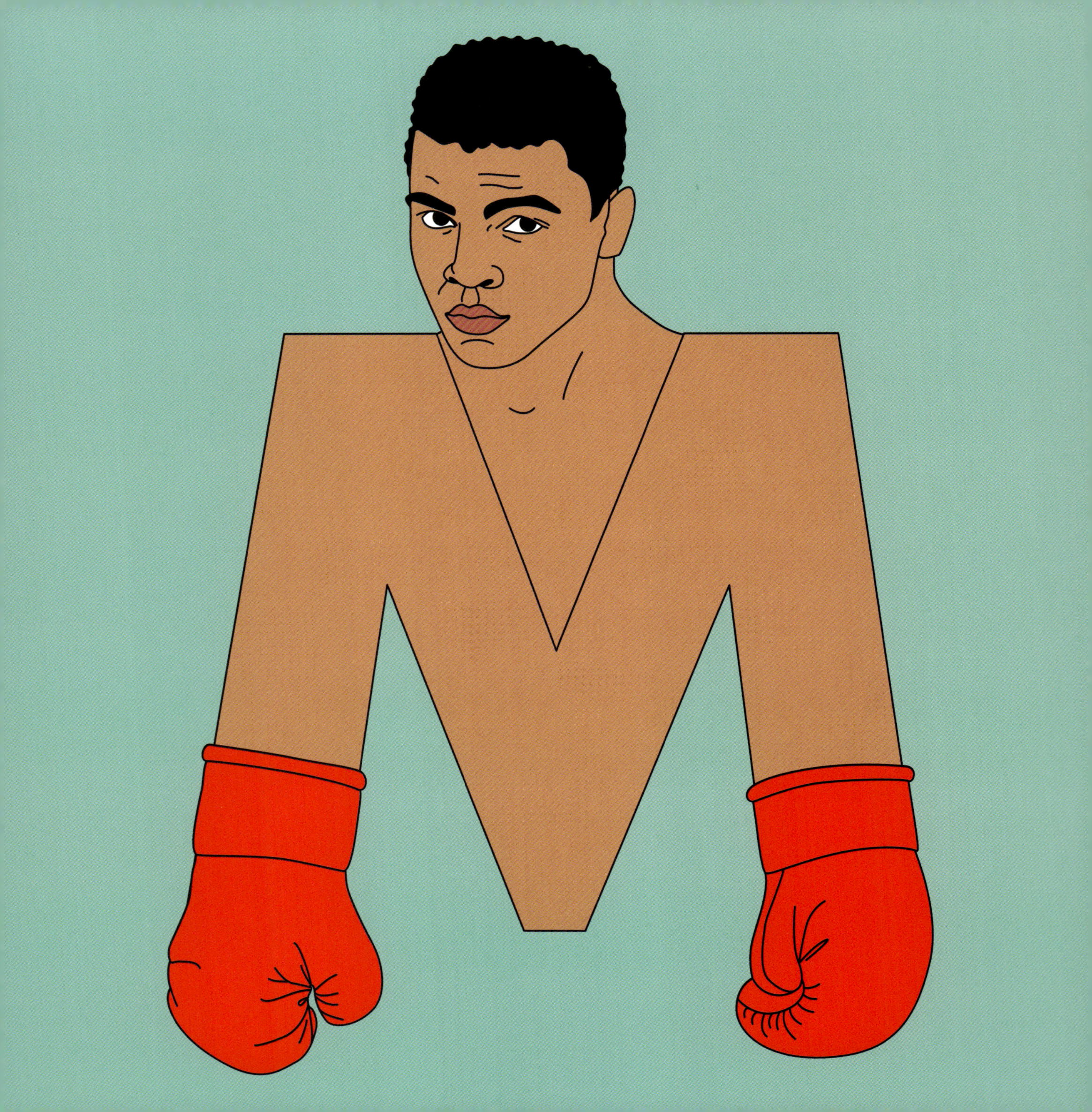

Mm

M is for Muhammad Ali.
'Float like a butterfly, sting like a bee.' When this three-time heavyweight champ refused to fight in the Vietnam War, he became a civil rights activist and a voice of Black pride. He was 'The Greatest' inside and outside the ring.

Nn

N is for **N**elson Mandela. South Africa's 'Father of the Nation' was a true freedom fighter. After 27 years in prison, he helped end the apartheid system. To crown his inspiring journey, he became the country's first president in 1994.

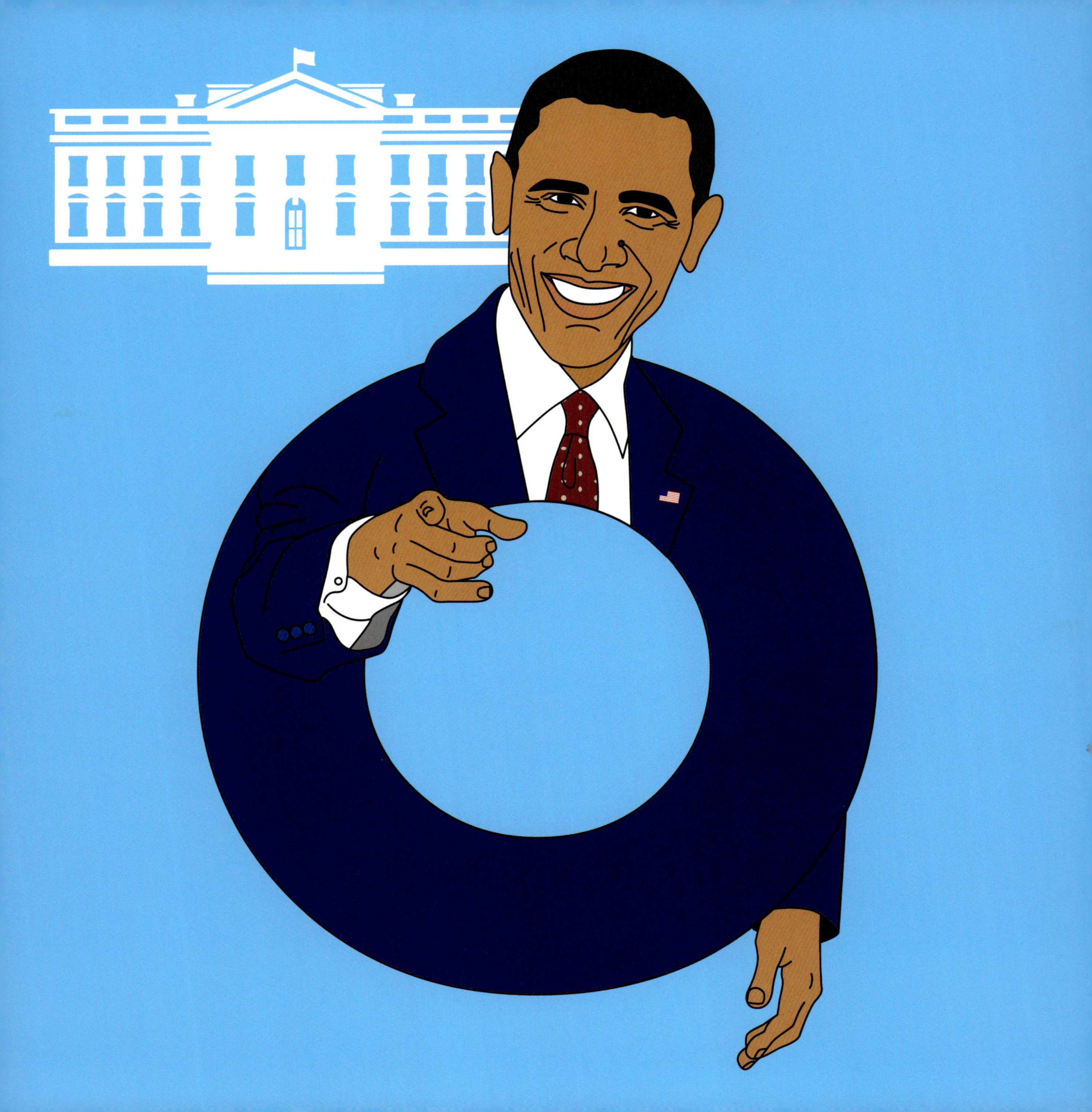

O is for Barack Obama. Nobel Peace Prize winner. Statesman. Writer. Activist. Healthcare reformer. This legend is famous for many things — but he will always be celebrated as the first Black President of the United States of America.

CLEVELAND AVE.
2857

P is for Rosa **P**arks.
'Never be fearful about what you are doing when it is right.'
In 1955, the 'First Lady of Civil Rights' refused to give up her seat on a bus to a white man. With that, she kick-started the civil rights movement in America.

Qq

Q is for **Q**uincy Jones.
With 28 Grammys to his name, this legend was one of the greatest record producers ever. He worked alongside Michael Jackson, arranged music for Sinatra, and was a producer for the 1985 version of 'The Color Purple.' He also contributed to countless Black charities.

ARCH
WASHINGTO

Rr

R is for Bayard Rustin.
Rustin was the main organizer of the March on Washington in 1963. Fifty years later, long after his death, Obama awarded this legendary civil rights and gay rights activist the Presidential Medal of Freedom.

S

Ss

S is for Sojourner Truth.
This New Yorker escaped slavery in 1826, then dedicated her life to fighting for abolition, Black rights, and women's rights. Her greatest moment came in 1851, when she delivered her speech, 'Ain't I a Woman?'

T is for Thurgood Marshall. 'Mr. Civil Rights' believed that the law is sacred. Once an NAACP lawyer, he won countless civil rights cases, battled segregation, and then, in 1967, became the first Black justice to serve on the Supreme Court!

U is for Ursula Burns.
'I was Black. I was a girl. And I was poor.' But that didn't stop her! After interning at Xerox, this legend rose through the company and became CEO — the first Black woman ever to lead a Fortune 500 company.

V is for Denmark **V**esey.
After buying his freedom from slavery in 1799, he planned an uprising to free as many slaves as he could. His plans may have failed, but Vesey will always be remembered as a hero for the way he dreamed of freedom for Black people in America!

NATIONAL ASSOCIATION FOR THE ADVANCEMENT OF COLORED PEOPLE
NAACP
FOUNDED
1909

W is for **W**.E.B. Du Bois.
As an author, intellectual, and founder of the NAACP, Du Bois fought for Black people's rights to schooling. In 1895, he became the first Black man to earn a PhD from Harvard, showing Black Americans that education was well within their reach.

X is for Malcolm **X**.
X was one of the key thinkers of the Black Power Movement. He pushed for Black pride, fought injustice, and delivered speeches that would stir the soul: 'You can't separate peace from freedom because no one can be at peace unless he has his freedom!'

Y

Yy

Y is for Andrew Young. Alongside leaders like MLK and John Lewis, this legend helped change America. After helping draft the Civil Rights Act, Young became the first Black man from Georgia elected to the U.S. House of Representatives since Reconstruction.

Zz

Z is for Zora Neale Hurston. With incredible talent and beautiful prose, Hurston wrote of the Black experience. Her novel, 'Their Eyes Were Watching God,' showed readers that Black people love, hurt, and feel just like everybody else. Today, it's remembered as an all-time classic.

The ever-expanding legendary library

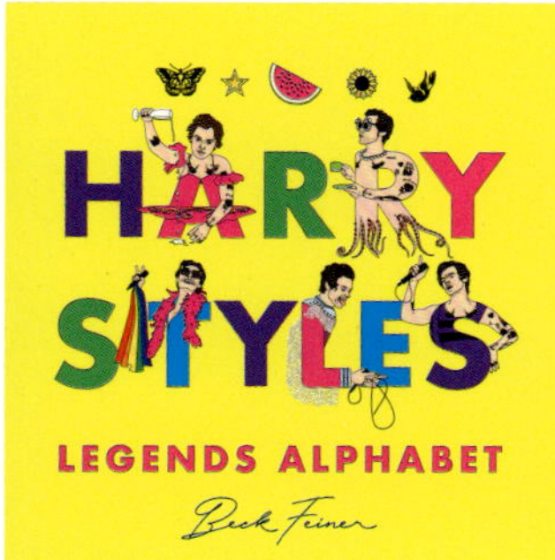

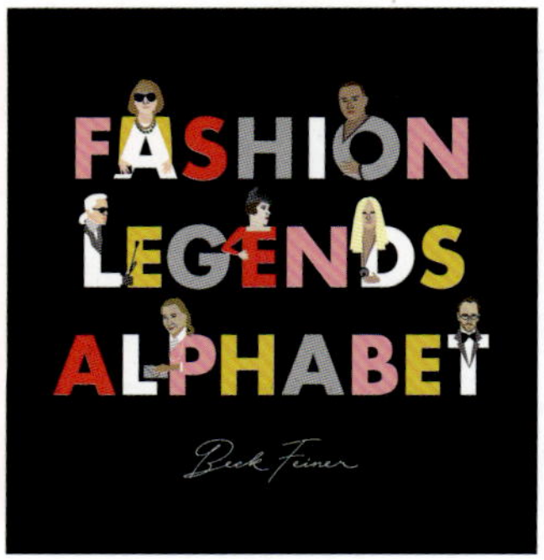

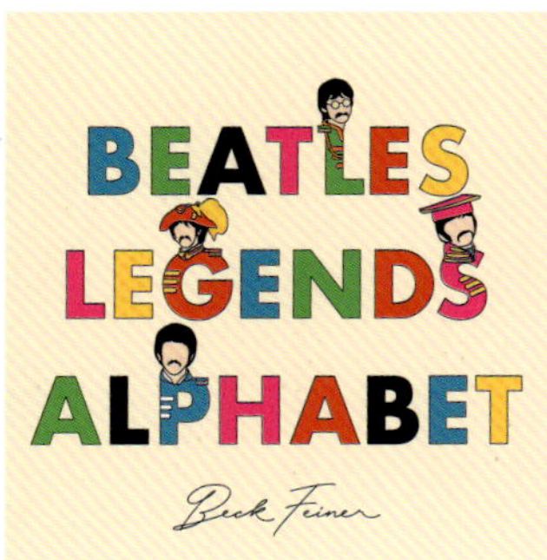

BLACK HISTORY LEGENDS ALPHABET

www.alphabetlegends.com

Published by Alphabet Legends Pty Ltd in 2024
Created by Beck Feiner

Printed and bound in China.

9780975669242

ALPHABET LEGENDS